God's Wonderful World

Photographed and hand painted by Kathleen Francour

Stories by Sylvia Seymour

Photography: © 1997 Kathleen Francour
Carefree, Arizona. All rights reserved.

ISBN: 0-7853-2119-5

PUBLICATIONS INTERNATIONAL, LTD.
7373 North Cicero Avenue
Lincolnwood, Illinois 60646

A Hill of Flowers

"Let's go play on the hill," said Tami, motioning to her best friend.

"Wait, Tami, wait!" called Rebecca.

Tami stopped and waited for Rebecca to catch up with her. At last they both stood at the top of the hill. The hill was covered with colorful flowers. How sweet they smelled!

"God made the flowers, didn't He?" asked Rebecca, leaning over to smell a daisy.

"Jesus must love us very much to give us such a wonderful place to play," Tami said.

Both children plopped to the ground. The grass tickled their bare toes. "Come on, Rebecca," said Tami, "let's roll down the hill! Weeeeeeee."

For rosy apples, juicy plums,
    And yellow pears so sweet,
For hips and haws on bush and hedge,
    And flowers at our feet,
For ears of corn all ripe and dry,
    And colored leaves on trees,
We thank You, heavenly Jesus Christ,
    For such good gifts as these.

Thank God for rain
and the beautiful rainbow colors.
And thank God for letting children
splash in puddles.

The Lord is good to me,
and so I thank the Lord
for giving me the things I need:
the sun, the rain, and the apple seed!
The Lord is good to me.

The New Kite

Mark ran as fast as he could. The kite bounced on the ground. Was it flying? No, just bouncing.

Mark could not understand. Dad had made his kite. It was the best kite in the whole world. It had a long tail. He had a big ball of string. He could run fast. Why wouldn't his kite fly?

Suddenly the kite bounced again and lifted up into the air. Mark held his string and watched the kite soar even higher. Mark knew that God made the wind. "Thank you, Jesus, for sending the wind to fly my kite!"

God bless the field and bless the lane,
　　Stream and branch and lion's mane,
Hill and stone and flower and tree,
　　From every end of my country—
Bless the sun and bless the sleet,
　　Bless the road and bless the street,
Bless the night and bless the day,
　　In each and every tiny way;
Bless the minnow, bless the whale,
　　Bless the rainbow and the hail,
Bless the nest and bless the leaf,
　　Bless the righteous and the thief,
Bless the wing and bless the fin,
　　Bless the air I travel in,
Bless the mill and bless the mouse,
　　Bless the miller's bricken house,
Bless the earth and bless the sea,
　　God bless you and God bless me.

God made the sun,
  And God made the trees.
God made the mountains,
  And God made me.

Thank you, O God,
  For the sun and the trees,
For making the mountains,
  And for making me.

The Colors in the Sky

Two children sat on a park bench watching the sun slowly slip down into the trees. "The sun is going to bed so the moon can come out to play," explained Terri.

The sky was blazing with bright orange, red, and pink. Jacob looked at his friend. "The sky looks like fire!" said Jacob pointing to the sunset. "Will it burn the moon?"

"It's not on fire, Jacob," said Terri. "God gives us beautiful colors at the end of the day to remember at night when the sky is dark."

"That's neat," said Jacob. "Thank you, Jesus, for making beautiful colors in the sky."

When the weather is wet,
　　We must not fret.
When the weather is cold,
　　We must not scold.
When the weather is warm,
　　We must not storm.
Be thankful together,
　　Whatever the weather.

Dear Jesus,
Who has made all things beautiful:
give me a love of Thy countryside, its lanes
and meadows, its woods and streams, and
clean open spaces; and let me keep it fresh and
unspoiled for those who shall come after me.

Amen.

Keep us, O Lord, as the apple of Your eye;
hide us under the shadow of Your wings.

When to the flowers so beautiful the Father gave a name,
  Back came a little blue-eyed one, all timidly she came.
And standing at the Father's feet and gazing in His face
  She said in low and trembling tones,
"Dear God, the name Thou gave to me, alas, I have forgot."
  Then kindly looked the Father down and said,
    "Forget Me not."